W9-CEI-413

Let's Be Social

Go to School

by L. L. Owens
illustrated by Chris Davidson

Content Consultant
M. A. Brennan
Assistant Professor, Community Development
Department of Family, Youth, and Community Sciences
University of Florida

magic wagon

visit us at www.abdopublishing.com

Published by Magic Wagon, a division of the ABDO Group, 8000 West 78th Street, Edina, Minnesota 55439. Copyright © 2011 by Abdo Consulting Group, Inc. International copyrights reserved in all countries. All rights reserved. No part of this book may be reproduced in any form without written permission from the publisher.

Looking Glass Library™ is a trademark and logo of Magic Wagon.

Printed in the United States of America, North Mankato, Minnesota.
012010
092010

♻ THIS BOOK CONTAINS AT LEAST 10% RECYCLED MATERIALS.

Text by L. L. Owens
Illustrations by Chris Davidson
Edited by Mari Kesselring
Interior layout and design by Becky Daum
Cover design by Becky Daum

Library of Congress Cataloging-in-Publication Data
Owens, L. L.
  Go to school / by L.L. Owens ; illustrated by Chris Davidson.
      p. cm. — (Let's be social)
  Includes index.
  ISBN 978-1-60270-799-3
  1. Schools—Juvenile literature. I. Davidson, Chris, 1974- ill. II. Title.
  LB1556.O84 2011
  371—dc22
                                        2009048351

Table of Contents

What Is a School?

Kids spend a lot of time at school. But what is a school? A school is a place where students learn. Teachers, staff, and students work and learn in a school. Every school is a community.

There are many different kinds of schools. Alex takes a bus to a public school. Some of his friends go to a private school nearby. Ashley is homeschooled. She learns from her mother at home.

SCHOOL

Places at School

Most of the school day is spent in a classroom. That is where Emma and her classmates learn new things.

Emma often sits at her desk. Sometimes she works at an art table. Emma keeps some of her things in a classroom closet.

Some schools have many classrooms. Others have only one classroom.

Brandon loves the school's gym. He goes there for gym class. It is a great place to exercise. He runs, plays soccer, and dances. He learns about teamwork while staying healthy.

Some schools have a music room. A class might go there to sing songs.

11

The playground is important to the school community. Sarah and Cody have recess on the playground. They play and relax with their classmates. On the weekend, they meet their friends there to play.

Paige and her friends eat lunch in the school's cafeteria. The cafeteria is also an auditorium. Paige performed in a play with her classmates there. At this school, the cafeteria, gym, and auditorium are all the same room.

People at School

The people at a school make up its community. The student community is made up of kids from all different backgrounds. The students are usually grouped by grade and divided into classroom groups. These small groups make up a larger school group.

A school might try to help out the community. Mara helps plant trees in the neighborhood with her classmates and teacher.

Mr. Hana's students work together. They support each other. This helps them reach learning goals. The class talks about the books they have read. They do math problems together.

Mr. Hana's students follow rules. They are helpful to each other and to Mr. Hana. Rules keep the community safe. That makes it easier to learn.

Ms. Collins is another teacher. Teachers at school support each other. They look out for their students.

Ms. Collins creates a plan for the subjects her students will study. The plan covers the whole school year. She gives her students extra help before and after school. Ms. Collins helps her students learn.

Mrs. Jones is the school's principal. She helps teachers do their jobs. She works with them to set school rules. She makes decisions about their classrooms. Mrs. Jones also gets to know the students. She is proud of their good work. If a student has a problem, she tries to help.

Who else works at a school? The school nurse takes care of students when they feel sick. The custodian keeps the school clean. The bus driver and the crossing guard help students get home after school.

Parents and other adults also help at the school. Some parents drop by to read stories to their child's class. A firefighter visits the school. He talks about fire safety.

STOP

SCHOOL

Everyone at school depends on each other. They work together toward the goal of learning. They have fun together. A school is a great community!

School Project

Write a letter to someone who helps make your school a better place. You can write to a teacher, a classmate, a parent, or anyone you like.

1. Choose a person. It should be someone you think helps your school community.

2. In your letter, tell the person why you have chosen him or her. Explain how the person improves your community. Be sure to say thank you.

3. Share your letter in class. Then deliver it to the person you wrote about.

Fun Facts

- Together, all the kids at one school are called the student body.

- The first schools in the United States were only one room. There were no separate grades.

- Millions of U.S. schoolchildren speak a language other than English. The majority of them speak Spanish.

Glossary

goal—something that a person works to accomplish.

homeschooled—to be formally educated at home.

staff—a group of people at a workplace.

support—to help and encourage someone.

teamwork—what happens when people do a task together.

On the Web

To learn more about schools, visit ABDO Group online at **www.abdopublishing.com**. Web sites about schools are featured on our Book Links page. These links are routinely monitored and updated to provide the most current information available.

Index